Sikh
Gurdwara

For Simran Singh

For a free color catalog describing Gareth Stevens' list of high-quality books and multimedia programs, call 1·800·542·2595 (USA) or 1·800·461·9120 (Canada). Gareth Stevens Publishing's Fax: (414) 225·0377.

Gareth Stevens Publishing thanks Mr. Surjit Singh (Zakhmi) for his assistance with the accuracy of the text. Mr. Singh is a Sikh priest in residence at the gurdwara of the Sikh Religious Society in Brookfield, Wisconsin.

Library of Congress Cataloging-in-Publication Data available upon request from publisher. Fax: (414) 225-0377 for the attention of the Publishing Records Department.

ISBN 0-8368-2610-8

This North American edition first published in 2000 by
Gareth Stevens Publishing
1555 North RiverCenter Drive, Suite 201
Milwaukee, WI 53212 USA

Original edition © 1998 by Franklin Watts.
First published in 1998 by Franklin Watts,
96 Leonard Street, London EC2A 4RH, England.
This U. S. edition © 2000 by Gareth Stevens, Inc.
Additional end matter © 2000 by Gareth Stevens, Inc.

Editor: Samantha Armstrong
Series Designer: Kirstie Billingham
Illustrator: Gemini Patel
Religious Education Consultant: Margaret Barratt, M.A., Religious Education lecturer and author
Sikh Consultant: Indarjit Singh OBE, Director of Network Sikh Organizations
Reading Consultant: Prue Goodwin, Reading and Language Information Centre, Reading

Gareth Stevens Series Editor: Dorothy L. Gibbs

Photographic acknowledgements:
Cover: Steve Shott Photography; Ann and Bury Peerless; p. 6 Ann and Bury Peerless; p. 7 Sikh Messenger Publications; p. 8 Ann and Bury Peerless; p. 9 Carlos Reyes-Manzo, Andes Press Agency; p. 17 Carlos Reyes-Manzo, Andes Press Agency. All other photographs by Steve Shott Photography.

With thanks to Khalsa Jatha, Shepherd's Bush Gurdwara.

Printed in the United States of America

1 2 3 4 5 6 7 8 9 04 03 02 01 00

PLACES OF WORSHIP

Sikh
Gurdwara

Kanwaljit Kaur-Singh

Gareth Stevens Publishing
MILWAUKEE

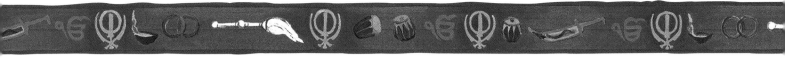

The khanda symbol is used to
represent the Sikh faith.

Contents

Words that appear in the glossary are printed in **boldface**
type the first time they occur in the text.

Gurdwaras around the World

A **gurdwara** is a place where Sikhs meet to worship
God. There are gurdwaras all around the world.
A gurdwara can be a room in a Sikh's home.

Sikh Beliefs

Sikhs believe in one God who was not born and will not die. The **Ik Onkar** sign means there is only one God. He is everywhere, all the time. Sikhs also believe that, because God created all of us, everyone is equal.

This sculpture is ▷
the Ik Onkar sign.

◁ This gurdwara
is in India.

The Gurus

A man called **Guru Nanak** started the Sikh religion in an area of India called **Punjab**. Nine other Gurus followed and taught Guru Nanak's teachings. *Guru* means "wise teacher" in the **Punjabi** language.

▲ There are often pictures of the Gurus in gurdwaras. Here, the nine Gurus who followed Guru Nanak are those seated on the mats around him.

Outside a Gurdwara

A flag called the **Nishan Sahib** flies outside every gurdwara. The **khanda** symbol in the middle of the flag is a sword, with sharp edges on both sides, inside a circle, and there are two more swords outside the circle. The circle means God is always present. The swords remind Sikhs to stand up for truth and to help those in need.

◁ The Nishan Sahib has the shape of a triangle and is an orange-yellow color called saffron.

Inside a Gurdwara

A gurdwara has a big hall that is used for worship. The holy Sikh book, the **Guru Granth Sahib**, is kept in this hall. A gurdwara also has a kitchen and a dining room, which is called a langar hall.

The Guru Granth ▷
Sahib is written
in Punjabi, which
is the language
of Sikhs.

The Guru Granth Sahib was written by the Gurus. In this holy book, hymns, called **shabads**, teach Sikhs about God and how to love and serve all God's people. A **chauri** is waved over the book to **respect** it.

Guru Granth Sahib

In the gurdwara, the Guru Granth Sahib rests on cushions on a platform with a canopy over it. When the holy book is closed, it is covered with beautiful cloths called **rumalas**. At the end of the day, it is carefully put away.

The Guru Granth Sahib is ▷ covered with rumalas when no one is reading it.

Showing Respect

When Sikhs enter a gurdwara, they take off their shoes and cover their heads. Then they bow or kneel in front of the Guru Granth Sahib to show their respect for the teachings of the Gurus.

◁ To show respect, these Sikh children are kneeling and bowing so their foreheads touch the floor.

Making an Offering

Offerings of food or money left in the gurdwara are used for people who need help.

◁ Even children put money into the collection box.

Worship in a Gurdwara

To worship in a gurdwara, everyone sits on the floor in front of the Guru Granth Sahib. The people at the service are called the congregation, or **sangat**.

Men and women usually sit on opposite sides of the big hall. In some gurdwaras, however, everyone sits together.

△ In this gurdwara, the
men and women are
sitting separately.

A Worship Service

During a worship service, the Guru Granth Sahib is read in Punjabi. Sometimes the reading is done by the **granthi** who works at the gurdwara. The granthi explains the reading and tells stories about the Gurus' lives. A Sikh priest is a granthi.

Before Guru Nanak's time, women were treated badly in India, and they were not allowed to worship with men. Guru Nanak taught that men and women are equal.

A Sikh woman is reading one ▷ of the shabads, or holy songs. She turns the pages of the Guru Granth Sahib very carefully.

Singing in a Service

During a service, the shabads from the Guru Granth Sahib are sung by people called **ragis**. Ragis also play the **harmonium** and Indian drums, called **tabla**.

Karah Prashad

At the end of a service, everyone eats a sweet food called the **Karah Prashad**. Eating together reminds Sikhs that all people are equal.

▽ Karah Prashad is a sweet paste made from sugar, butter, flour, and water.

After a Service

After a worship service in the gurdwara, everybody eats together in the langar hall. The food served is called **langar**.

△ The food is vegetarian, never meat, so everyone can enjoy it.

◁ The langar is cooked and served by both men and women. Sikh men and women share the responsibilities of housework and looking after the family.

22

Sikhs wear five special things as signs of their faith. The name of each one begins with the letter *k*, so they are called the "five *ks*." The five *ks* were started by the tenth Guru, Guru Gobind Singh.

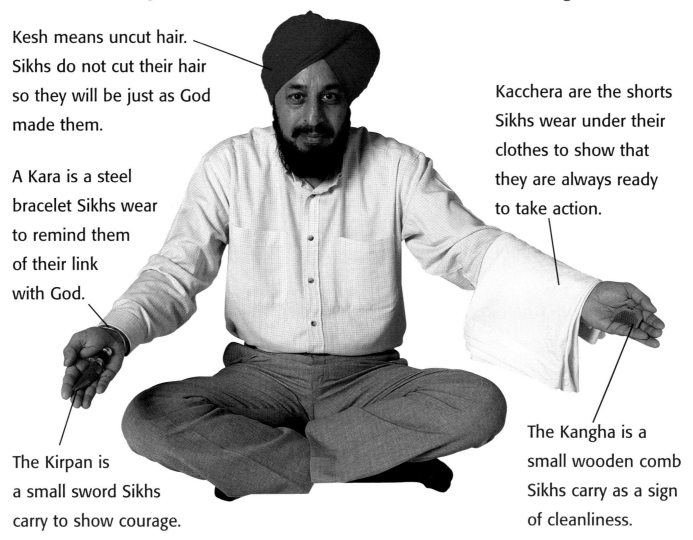

Kesh means uncut hair. Sikhs do not cut their hair so they will be just as God made them.

A Kara is a steel bracelet Sikhs wear to remind them of their link with God.

Kacchera are the shorts Sikhs wear under their clothes to show that they are always ready to take action.

The Kirpan is a small sword Sikhs carry to show courage.

The Kangha is a small wooden comb Sikhs carry as a sign of cleanliness.

24

Sikh Dress

Sikhs must keep their hair neat and clean, and it must be covered at the gurdwara. Sikh men and boys often wear **turbans** or **patkas** to cover their hair. Sikh women wear a long scarf called a **chunni**.

Young boys wear a ▷ patka to cover their hair. A patka looks like a small turban.

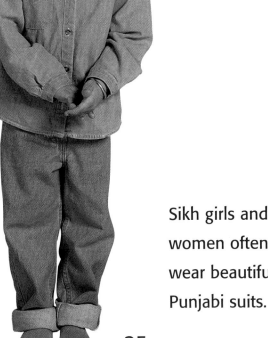

Sikh girls and ▷ women often wear beautiful Punjabi suits.

School in a Gurdwara

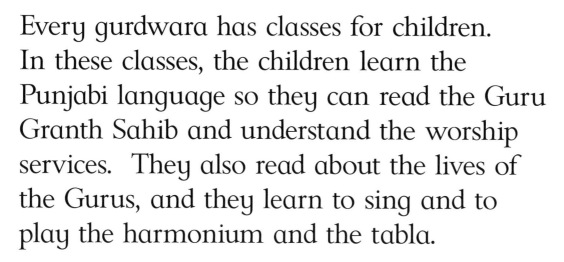

Every gurdwara has classes for children. In these classes, the children learn the Punjabi language so they can read the Guru Granth Sahib and understand the worship services. They also read about the lives of the Gurus, and they learn to sing and to play the harmonium and the tabla.

Children help around the gurdwara, too. Helping others is called **sewa**. By helping, children learn the Sikh way of life.

Glossary

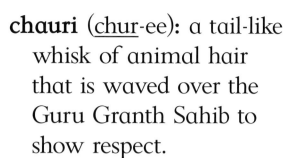

chauri (<u>chur</u>-ee): a tail-like whisk of animal hair that is waved over the Guru Granth Sahib to show respect.

chunni (<u>chew</u>-nee): the long scarf Sikh women wear to cover their heads in a gurdwara.

granthi (<u>grahn</u>-tee): a worker in a gurdwara who reads the Guru Granth Sahib; a Sikh priest.

gurdwara (gur-<u>dwah</u>-rah): a place where Sikhs meet to worship God.

guru (goo-roo): a wise teacher; a spiritual guide.

Guru Granth Sahib: the Sikh holy book.

Guru Nanak: the first Sikh guru, who started the Sikh religion.

harmonium: an Indian musical instrument that has a small keyboard.

Ik Onkar (Eek <u>Ahn</u>-ker): the Sikh symbol for one God.

Karah Prashad (Kah-rah Prah-<u>sahd</u>): a sweet food Sikhs share at the end of a worship service to remind them that everyone is equal.

khanda (<u>kahn</u>-da): the symbol on the Sikh flag.

langar (<u>lahn</u>-gur): the food eaten by everyone after a Sikh worship service.

Nishan Sahib (Nee-<u>sahn</u> <u>Sah</u>-eeb): the triangular-shaped, saffron-colored Sikh flag that flies outside every gurdwara.

patka (<u>paht</u>-kah): the turbanlike piece of material Sikh boys wear to cover their uncut hair.

Punjab (Poon-<u>job</u>): the place in India where the Sikh religion began.

Punjabi (Poon-<u>job</u>-ee): the language spoken in the Punjab area.

ragis (<u>rah</u>-jees): Sikh musicians who sing shabads from the Guru Granth Sahib.

respect: to treat with honor and thoughtful consideration.

rumalas (room-<u>ah</u>-lahs): the cloths used to cover the Guru Granth Sahib.

sangat (<u>sahn</u>-ghot): a congregation, or gathering, of Sikhs at a worship service.

sewa: helping others.

shabads (shah-<u>bahds</u>): hymns found in the Guru Granth Sahib.

tabla (<u>tah</u>-blah): a pair of small Indian drums.

turban: the long piece of material Sikh men wear to cover their uncut hair.

More Books to Read

The Children of India. World's Children (series). Jules Hermes (First Avenue Editions)

India. Countries of the World (series). Michael S. Dahl (Bridgestone Books)

India. Country Fact Files (series). Anita Ganeri (Raintree/Steck-Vaughn)

India. Festivals of the World (series). Falaq Kagda (Gareth Stevens)

Religion. Eyewitness Books (series). Myrtle Langley (Knopf)

Sikh. Beliefs and Cultures (series). Catherine Chambers (Children's Press)

Sikh Festivals. Celebrate (series). John Coutts (Heineman Library)

Sikhism. Discovering Religions (series). Sue Penney (Raintree/Steck-Vaughn)

Sikhism. World Religions (series). Kanwaljit Kaur-Singh (Thomson Learning)

What Do We Know About Sikhism? What Do We Know About...? (series). Beryl Dhanjal (Peter Bedrick Books)

Worlds of Belief: Religion and Spirituality. Our Human Family (series). Lisa Sita (Blackbirch)

Videos

Families of India.
(Library Video)

How Do You Spell God?
(HBO Kids Video)

*Windows to the World:
India* (IVN
Entertainment)

Web Sites

Being a Sikh
*www.sikhmuseum.org/
bs.htm*

Juniors@SIKH.net
*www.sikh.net/Juniors/
index.htm*

Learn to Read Punjabi
*www.innotts.co.uk/
~ukindia/zpun01.htm*

Pictures of Historical
Gurduaras
*roscoe.bu.edu/~rajwi/
sikhgifs/*

Sikhnet: Youth and Children
*www.sikhnet.com/s/
Youth+And+Children*

Young Khalsa Home Page
www.youngkhalsa.org

To find additional web sites, use a reliable search engine with one
or more of the following keywords: *gurdwara, guru, Guru Granth
Sahib, Nishan Sahib, Punjab, ragi, shabad, Sikh,* and *Sikhism.*

Index